Our Brother Jim

by Lloyd J. Stefanic

DORRANCE PUBLISHING CO
EST. 1920
PITTSBURGH, PENNSYLVANIA 15238

Dorrance Publishing Co
585 Alpha Drive
Pittsburgh, PA 15238
Visit our website at *www.dorrancebookstore.com*

ISBN: 979-8-88925-018-0
eISBN: 979-8-88925-518-5

Preface

I am writing this book to honor our brother Jim and to make afflicted people aware that they can do much more than society expects of them. Don't be afraid or feel sorry for yourself.

Jim had cerebral palsy, retardation, could not speak and was not supposed to live past the age of three according to the doctors. Jim lived to the age of seventy-four even though he never walked until he was eight, could never date or get married, play sports, or go to school like normal people.

Yet, through our parents' devotion, care, and never-ending love, he achieved doing many things most people could not even attempt given his conditions.

Actual events, accomplishments and personal feelings are entered here without the influence of being politically correct, just factual.

I often wonder if Jim were normal just what he could have done and what accomplishments he would have achieved.

Sign Language

- Form his hands in a circle to indicate pizza
- Hold his hands about a foot apart for a cheesesteak sandwich
- Pull on the corner of his eyes for Chinese food
- Cup his hand like holding a cup for a drink, separate one hand above the other for a can of soda (coke)
- Place his hands together to the side of his head and tilt his head to go to bed
- Put his hands in a praying position to indicate the priest, who came to visit Jim and our mother, to give him Communion. (He learned to bless himself.)
- Point to his wrist where watch would be for time, usually indicating you were late, which he used to do to the priest when he came at different times
- Indicate a petting motion for a dog
- Put his hands aside and shrug his shoulders indicating he didn't know
- Put his fingers apart and hold his hands above his head for a deer
- Hunting - Indicate shooting a rifle
- Fishing - Indicate casting a rod
- Roll his hand over his face for getting washed
- Hold his hands up and make noises when you didn't understand what he wanted

- Show steering for a car
- Indicate using a mop for the cleaning lady
- Indicate a height for the kids
- Indicates long hair for a girl
- Pumping his arm to indicate blowing the trucks horn
- Showing his hands praying then point away if Mom, Dad, and our sister went to church
- Show praying and pointing to his mouth that the priest gave him Holy Communion
- Make a face if you gave him something he didn't like
- Motion of squeezing for a bottle of ketchup or mustard
- Cutting and poking for a knife and fork, stir for a spoon
- Pretend to shoot a basketball or swing like a bat to tell you what he watched on TV
- Point to the TV to turn it off
- Put his hand to his chin if someone had a beard (He loved people with beards.)
- Hold his nose for a bad odor or smell
- Hold his forehead or stomach if he or someone in the house was sick
- Hand over his heart if someone passed away
- Army salute for twin brother John
- Jim did not like airplanes. He would hold his arms apart like wings on a plane then shake his head no.
- Hold his hands apart and turn like driving a motorcycle when he had used the snowmobile
- Point to dishes to be put away
- Point to light or lamp to turn on or off
- Indicate sweating when he's hot
- Indicate shivering when he's cold

Prologue

Our father was born and raised in Western Pennsylvania where, as a young man, he worked in the coal mines with his father. When mining was slow there, they went to upstate Pennsylvania in the Scranton area to work in the coal mines there going back and forth for years. During their stay in Scranton, he traveled down to Philadelphia, not sure why, but there he met our mother. After they got married, they settled upstate in Troop, Pennsylvania, still working in the mines. Our father hunted up there with his buddies and later after moving back down to Philly he purchased a lot near where they hunted. Not caring for city life too much, he built a house on that lot that we still own. As kids, we spent the whole summer up there with our mother while our father came up every weekend after work.

Jim loved it up there. He was more relaxed and happier being up there. When we returned to Philly to go back to school, he would always point indicating he wanted to go back there.

Our parents were with Jim all day their entire lives. The only time they were apart was when our father was at work or hunting when Jim was small. My mother was with him almost every minute of his life. Only when Jim was in school and the one time our mother went to Europe with sister Ann were the only times they were not together.

I feel this constant companionship was very soothing and relaxing for Jim that someone was always there and what led Jim to live longer, not what the doctor predicted.

I feel that growing up and living with Jim influenced me to view people differently than most people i.e., being drawn to people with disabilities and feel they are more genuine probably because they can't do or don't put on the airs, some distain to normal people who claim they can't do something without even trying, since I viewed Jim's determination to do normal things and his expression and smile when he achieved his goal. Simple things like watching him putting coins in the slot of his piggy bank. He had little control over his hands, and it took a long time of him trying, and when he got one in there was that big smile and a grunt of satisfaction. But he was that way with all things that we take for granted since it was so easy for us but a big accomplishment for him.

When we were younger, I remember our parents would take us to the "lakes", a park located near were we lived in the city. My most vivid memory was when we were there one time by the lake and our father pointed to some fish swimming near the shore. Jim bent over to look, lost his balance, and fell in the water. Jim went under and father jumped in and pulled him out. He was soaking wet, shaking, and extremely upset. After they got him calmed down and dried off, we went home. He was still upset at home for a long time. That incident evidently scared him so much he would never go close to the water from the fear of that event.

Growing up, Jim was very modest. He would not let anyone see him in his underwear. He would peek out of his bedroom door to see if anyone were around before scurrying into the bathroom.

I have no idea of how this developed, but it did and went on for the years until he could not get to the bathroom anymore. After Mother passed away, he became incapacitated, confined to a wheelchair, and allowed my sister and me to change him, wipe his behind and put him to bed.

He apparently accepted the fact that he was no longer capable of doing normal things, that he worked so hard to accomplish over the years and allowed us to care for his needs.

I'm sure he was embarrassed but never let it on to us. He just accepted the fact that he was no longer capable and needed help.

Our Brother Jim

Jim and his twin brother John were born on October 28, 1941 with Jim emerging seven minutes after John with the doctor using forceps to remove Jim from our mother's womb.

In addition to being born with cerebral palsy and retardation, the use of the forceps damaged Jim's vocal cords leaving him unable to speak but only to make sounds.

Jim never walked until he was eight years old with my father carrying him everywhere we went over all those years. When he did walk, it was very noticeable. It took a lot of effort on his part that was not normal since he would drag his one leg. He would fall a lot, especially when he tried to run, wanting to be able to do so like us. Even though the doctors said his retardation was that of a five-year-old, Jim was very mechanically inclined. He loved to play with trucks and would align them into different positions when playing with them.

2

Jim, like the other retarded people, had this perception that everything had to be put back in its original place where my parents had
them. If you used something and did not put it where it belonged, he
would get your attention and point to the object you moved and point
to where it belonged for you to put it there.

Jim loved to eat and had his favorites; since he couldn't speak, he
would let you know what he wanted by pointing to what you showed
him what we had to eat. If he did not like any of that, he would do his
sign language for pizza, steak sandwich, etc. You got a big smile when
you gave him the thumbs up.

When we were kids, we would take a broken roller skate apart
and nail the front and back portion to a four-foot piece of two-by-
four. Then nail a wooden milk box to the front with two strips of
wood on top for the handlebars. We made one for Jim and he would
go all over the neighborhood with it after he learned to ride it. Just
by the smile on his face you knew how much he appreciated it. With
people around he would point to the scooter then point to Johnny
and me indicating we made it for him.

We used to go to the recreation center (Greenwich) to play baseball, basketball, swimming, and ping pong. The guys who kept score
and the time clock for basketball taught Jim to start and stop the clock

when they signaled to him. Jim loved doing it and in turn he learned to like basketball over the years. I took him to see the Harlem Globetrotters play and he smiled, laughed, and pointed to them the whole time. In time Jim learned to go to the rec center to do the clock on his own.

Jim loved to play with toy trucks; he would line them up and play with them for hours. Down the block where we lived was the Liquid Carbonic plant who had a lot of trucks. Jim would go down there to look at the trucks. Somehow the truck drivers figured out how much Jim enjoyed being around the trucks. They started taking him with them on their delivery runs, buying him lunch then bringing him home. Once again Jim was in all his glory.

Even when we were up in the Pocono Mountains in our old house a truck driver, Gary, who we knew growing up would take Jim on his travels. Gary told us he would point to the number on the clock to tell Jim when he would be leaving on his next trip and Jim would be on time.

Jim and money. Somewhere along the way Jim learned about money and the value of it. He would hide the money he got from Christmas, birthdays, and what he made pumping gas at the gas station in his bedroom. The guys at the gas station let him pump the gas and then would motion to stop pumping the gas.

When we would kid with him showing him our money, he would laugh and indicate, by separating his fingers, showing us how high his piles of money were. Then point to me and separate his fingers higher indicating that I had more money than him. He was tight with his money.

Our father was a hunter, and every year he and his hunting buddies would spend a week deer hunting in our Pocono house. I hunted with my father and his gang, and when I got time, I would hunt the whole week too. Jim always showed his interest about hunting even though he could not use a gun or travel through the woods.

When my father realized he wanted to go along, he brought him with us for the week.

Even though he could not hunt, just being there with the hunting gang provided much pleasure for him. He would even get up early when we did to have breakfast with us. Breakfasts were great; most of the guys were World War II vets with one being a cook in the Army and another a Navy cook. They took turns making breakfast and always tried to outdo the other. When we left to go into the woods to hunt, Jim would clean up without being asked to, doing all the dishes, pots, pans, etc. He did a good job! We assume he learned by watching our mother doing the dishes at home.

When someone got a deer and dragged it back to the cabin, Jim would help in hanging it from the tree out back with a smile because I guess that was how he could participate. After watching Jim for years while hunting, I could tell he always wanted to do more. Years later after a lot of my father's gang could not hunt anymore, I happened to get a big eight-pointer. I drug it most of the way back to the cabin. I then left the deer, went to the cabin, got Jim telling him to come with me.

When Jim saw the big rack, he got very excited. I then got him to help me drag the deer back to the cabin. He was elated because I guess that made him feel like he was participating now in a deer hunt. From that day until the time we lost Jim, he would hold his hands spread over his head to indicate the deer antlers and then hold his hands over his shoulder, pulling the way he helped to drag the deer. To me that was his biggest thrill ever, because I got that deer mounted and had it on the wall in my house. When he was there and any one of my friends or family members were there, Jim would point to the deer and show them that he helped me drag it out of the woods.

With our father's deer

Deer Jim helped to drag out of the woods

Jim loved dogs. We always had beagles since my father grew up with them and always used them to hunt small game. He always petted them, and they were always climbing into his lap or lying beside him. He always grinned at them and I feel that was because they made him feel relaxed and they were not afraid of him.

Jim with a beagle

With beagle

Our parents in time started teaching Jim to eat with a spoon and fork; he was never able to use a knife. They would cut his meat up for him, knowing he would wind up hurting himself. He was unsteady with the utensils and his food would go all over the table and us.

I particularly remember him splashing peas into my plate and my father telling us not to react to it because Jim would get all upset, thereby making it harder for him to learn to control the utensils. In time he learned to eat okay by himself, but never using a knife. But there would still be times that food went all over causing him to get upset with himself. However, over time everything worked out for the best. He could never master buttering his own bread.

Our mother was a very kind and patient woman, very dedicated to making Jim feel at ease. She always tried to make things as easy as possible for him. Jim was aware that he was not normal and would get upset and nervous if people stared or laughed at him, which they did. Our mother always managed to get him calmed down. At times while outside, some of the kids would tease or make fun of him.

The one incident that sticks out in my mind was when we were eating out at a restaurant. The lady at a few tables away with her family kept staring at Jim even pointing to him and then saying things to the others are her table. It got to a point where Jim got so upset, he would not eat or look up because they kept it up for so long. This was the first time I saw our mother ever confront anyone. But she got up, went over to their table, and blasted them for being so ignorant in upsetting a handicapped person to a point where he couldn't eat. Needless to say, she embarrassed them to a point where they did not look over anymore, finished eating then quickly left.

Jim was obsessed with the dirty dishes being around. If you were done eating and got up without taking your dish to the sink, he would grunt at you, point to your dish and then to the sink. Everything had to be picked up and put away right away. If everything wasn't picked up or put away to his liking, he would do it. Even to start washing the dishes if they weren't done fast enough for him. Everything had to be put back where it belonged and the dishes had to be washed, dried, and put away before you could go watch TV or do something else. Even if you left something out of place in another room, he would get your attention for you to put it where it belonged.

Jim used certain signs and motions to describe someone or what someone was doing or where they were. If we were looking for our father and he wasn't around, Jim would indicate he was at work by swinging his arms as though using a hammer. He would use his arms as though shooting a rifle if he were hunting or shrug his shoulder if he didn't know. Washing or drying actions of a plate was the sign for our mother. He used the Army salute for his twin brother, John, as John was in the Army. Sister Ann by pointing to his hair because she went to the hairdresser every week. Our priest by holding his hands as praying. The dogs by holding his hands low to show its height and a petting motion. Showing the motion of cutting scissors and pointing to the back of his neck was for a haircut. If he saw something, he would point to his eyes, if he smelled something he would hold his nose, but he never pointed to his ears, so we weren't sure about his hearing. He would put his hands together, against his cheek if he was ready for bed. His favorite was holding his fingers over his head and point to his eyes. That was if he saw a deer.

I remember on occasion, when I would go visit our father, Jim showed me his hammer motion and then moving his fingers indicating dad was making money working. Then I pointed to him to hammer and make money. He looked at me and laughed, shrugged his shoulders, and put his hands apart as though telling me he couldn't.

One day when I was in my backyard, my next-door neighbor came over and said, "Your brother embarrassed me."

I said, "My brother John? What did he do?"

He said, "No, Jimmy."

"How?" I asked.

He told me he was trying to get his lawnmower started to cut his grass and it wouldn't kick over. Jim was walking by, came over and was watching him. He said it would not start. Then, Jim reached down, pressed the choke and the mower started. Jim smiled, waved, and walked off.

Jim always watched our father working on his car or lawn mower, so I guess he knew what to do in some cases. I remember one time changing the spark plugs on my car and Jim was there watching me. I started looking where I put the spark plug gauge. Jim grunted at me and pointed to it, knowing exactly what I was looking for.

Watching our father work on car

Jim learned all about tools watching our father working on something. It got to a point that by observing, even though he could never master using any tool because of his unsteadiness, he knew which tool he was going to use next, and he would hand it to him.

Our father bought a snowmobile and somehow taught Jim how to drive it. They lived by a big field on the electric companies' powerline and that's where he drove it. Jim looked forward for snow so he could drive it around. The look on his face when he was on it showed how much this small achievement brought him so much happiness that he could drive something too. I can still visualize how happy and upbeat he was driving it around.

On snowmobile

In 1945 our father built a cabin in the Pocono mountains where he hunted deer and bear. We stayed there all summer until school started in the fall. There was an outhouse, no electricity, or running water.

At the Pocono house

We had a wood/coal stove to cook on. A rain barrel to catch the rainwater to wash dishes. Kerosene lamps for light at night. John and I would take our wagon with two metal milk containers down to the lake where the icehouse* was located with a well, fill them up then haul them back to the cabin.

Of course, going there was downhill so pulling the filled milk container uphill was a chore. This water was for our drinking and cooking. Many years later we had a well drilled and built a coal bin outside and a small shed outback.

We picked blueberries, blackberries, played ball on the road, fished and swim at the lake. At night we all played cards with the kerosene lamps for light. Jim would go to the lake with us, and we would help him fish. When he caught a fish, he was elated, grinning from ear to ear.

He never tried or would go into the water when we swam. Jim seemed the happiest up there and was more relaxed. When we played cards, he would look over our shoulder and we would point to a card we were going to play. He would shake his head yes like he knew what he was doing. Sometimes we would hand him the card to lay down.

At the farm, across the road from our cabin, we used to buy our eggs. Their son had two young girls who used to bake cookies. One day Jim went with me to the farm and they offered him a cookie. He ate the cookie, gave them a big smile, and they gave him more. Well, that started a relationship with them that every time they made cookies, Jim got his share.

After the girls got married and moved away, Jim would shrug his shoulders, indicating he didn't get his usual delivery of cookies anymore.

Sometimes brother John and I would take Jim down to the lake, and there John and I would hunt for water snakes. We never indicated to him about hunting for water snakes because Jim did not like snakes. When Jim realized what we were doing, he would walk further back from the lake and sit down.

If we caught one, we would take it to show Jim and he would grab a stick and wave it at us. It was unclear if the stick was for the snake or us! Back at the cabin, he would move his hands like a slithering snake to our parents and point to us. We got in trouble.

Where our cabin was located, there was a lot of blueberry bushes. At the end of July, the blueberries were in full bloom and ready for picking. We had one and two pound coffee cans with a rope attached to hang around our neck that allowed us to use both hands to pick the berries. We looked forward to picking them be- cause our mother made us pies and muffins. She also put the blue- berries in our cereal at breakfast.

In time, Jim indicated he wanted to pick the berries too. To make it easier for him, we gave him the bigger coffee can to put the berries in and led him to the bushes that were more plentiful. We showed him to only pick the blue ones.

Jim had a difficult time since he couldn't control his fingers for proper picking. It was hard for him to be gentle enough so to not crush the soft, ripe berries. He crushed most of them but managed to get some into his pail. Even though we would pick much more, he seems content that he was able to pick with us and accomplish another challenge. His hands and clothes would be all spotted purple from all the berries he crushed but it didn't stop him from wanting to pick the berries. When we returned to the cabin, our parents would smile at his pail and pat him on his back which always got a smile from Jim.

When we were back home in Philly and would be getting ready to go back upstate, we would point going up there and he always nodded yes to go. Later after our father passed away and people from New York bought the house next to us, knocked it down and started to build another house, they kept getting stopped for violations, and then left it abandoned with a partially built concrete basement, high weeds, and trash around. Jim would point over there and shake his head no; hold his hands in the air and shrug his shoulders indicating he did not like seeing that. It stayed that way for about fifteen years.

A few years after the initial stoppage of building and nothing being done next door, Jim would shake his head no when I was going back upstate. The property being left like that bothered him so much that he never wanted to go back to a place he loved so much.

I often wonder if our parents and Jim had moved back up there how it would have affected him seeing that mess every day.

The shed father built in the back was to store our mower and tools. The shed was up against some large rocks in the rear and the shed had a slightly slanted roof. We don't know how, but Jim managed to get onto the roof and sit up there. One day Jim was sitting on the roof, and I don't recall why but I started teasing him. Jim got so mad at me that he leaned back to far, fell off the roof and hit his head on the rocks. Jim was bleeding, Mother screamed, and I got the beating of my life.

To this day I can still visualize him falling and all the problems I caused. Jim wound up with a scar on his head; he would point to it then point to me.

When Jim went fishing with us off the icehouse pier, and if he hooked a fish, he would hand us the fishing pole to bring the fish in. At times he would pull to hard the fish would get off and occasionally we got hit with the pole. He would laugh at us ducking out of the way and be thrilled to death if he hauled it in and we got the fish off the hook and into the bucket.

Basically, he was afraid of water and would always shake his head no when we tried to get him into the rowboat. He used to watch us swim, so I figured he knew he wasn't capable of swimming and was satisfied just to watch us.

While with us deer hunting, if someone had missed a deer and was telling everyone their story back at the cabin, Jim would watch intently. Apparently, he knew what they did or were saying because he would look and point to that person and laugh and shrug his shoulders. One time when I had taken a deer, he looked at that guy and pointed to me that I got one. I guess he was telling them they were a bad shot. The rest of the guys jumped on the bandwagon pointing at him as a bad shooter and gave him the thumbs down. Jim really got a big kick out of that kibbitzing.

The icehouse was a high wooden structure a couple of hundreds of yards long. They stored blocks of ice in there that were cut from the frozen lake, in the winter, and had a conveyor belt that hauled the ice blocks up and into the icehouse for storage. Those blocks of ice were loaded in refrigerator railroad cars that stopped there by wheel barrels.

3

When we lived in South Philly, our neighbor, who lived two doors from us, had a nephew who was afflicted and put in a home. He seemed to feel that Jim should have been put in a home as well. He always made these comments and did not want Jim near his house for some reason or another. It got to a point where Johnny and I would have to sit outside to watch Jim until our father got home from work.

Then our neighbor got a puppy. They kept the puppy on the front porch. Johnny and I apparently got distracted and Jim went up on the porch to pet the puppy. Mr. – came out of the house and pushed Jim down the porch steps, which were concrete.

Our mother was cleaning up Jim's scrapes and cuts when our father got home. He asked what happened, and we told him. He put his lunch pail down, turned around, and went out of the house. We followed him. The neighbors were in the house eating their supper; my father went into their house, dragged the father from the table through the house, and threw him down the steps.

All the neighbors knew what happened and were all outside to see what was going to happen. When our father tossed him down the steps, they all cheered and clapped their hands, happy that he got his due. From that time on, we never had a problem with them again.

Our father told us that sometimes you have to go down to other people's level to get your point across. But only as a last resort. Unfortunately, our neighbor learned that lesson the hard way.

Many years later while at work, I got a coffee from the cafeteria and was walking back to my desk. A man was servicing the vending machine in the hallway. He called my name, but I did not recognize him. He was the son of the neighbor who pushed Jim down the steps. The first thing he said to me was, "How is Jimmy?" I felt that gesture indicated to me that he never approved of his father's feelings about Jim.

One morning when we were eating breakfast, Jim came into the kitchen and plopped a stack of money in the front of sister Ann. Everyone looked at him in amazement and he pointed his finger toward the front door and then shrugged his shoulders. He motioned for us to follow him and he led us outside and showed us a dent in Ann's car fender.

Here, Jim had been taking her car keys, and when no one was around or sleeping, he would drive her car around the block and then re-park it. The reason we determined this was because her car would be parked in different spots and she would always say she didn't remember parking it there.

He apparently gave her the money to pay for the damage. I still find it hard to believe that with his condition and lack of control of his limbs that he could ever learn how to drive let alone do it.

Near our house were a couple factories. One was a bleach factory about a block away. At that time empty soda bottles would be returned for a few pennies. When the workers finished their lunch, they would leave the empty soda bottles around the inside and outside of the factory.

As kids we would collect the bottles to get the refund. The worker would tell all us kids where they left them inside and we would go in and get them. On day Jim was with some of the kids inside the factory and the owner happened to be there and called the police.

When they saw the cops, they all ran except for Jim who couldn't run and was unaware of what the cops do, had been in the factory many times before and didn't realize what was going on. The police handcuffed Jim, took him to the police station, booked him, then called my father to come get him. I have no idea how the police knew how to get a hold of our father. We assumed the cops knew who he was and where he lived to be able to call our father.

The factory owner pressed charges against Jim so they had to book him. From what we found out later, some of the kids were apparently stealing bottles of bleach along with getting the empty soda bottles and the owner knew it. The owner filed charges and Jim had to appear in court.

Our father had to take off from work the day of the hearing to take Jim to court. At the hearing, the owner stated the kids used to steal bleach and he wanted to prosecute Jim, the only one the cops caught. When the judge summoned Jim to appear before him, the judge watched Jim walk up with our father and he asked Jim how he pleaded. My father explained to the judge that he couldn't speak and about his disabilities. The judge then looked at the factory owner and asked him if he still wanted to press charges and he said "yes". The judge stared at him, raised his gavel, banged it on his desk and said case dismissed.

Jim would later indicate a cop by holding his fingers in a circle over his wrist, then hold his hands indicating the way he was handcuffed.

As kids in the Poconos, we didn't have a TV, so we played a lot of card games (mostly war) at night. Since Jim wasn't able to play, he would sit behind us and watch. In time, if Jim was behind me when it was my turn to play a card, I would pull it up show Jim the card and he would shake his head yes, like he knew that I should play that card, so I played that card. If I took the trick, he would smile and laugh. If

I lost the trick, I would look at him and he would put his hands up and shrug his shoulders like "oh well". I would make a face at him and he would laugh. But in the end, it made him feel like he was playing too.

If Jim got mad at you or vice versa, when he got over it, he would motion for you to come over, then hold out his hand and shake yours. I would shake his hand then stick my tongue out at him and he would laugh knowing I was kidding and that everything was okay.

None of us were heavy, as a matter of fact we were all skinny. A couple of houses down from us were two girls who were heavy. To this day I still don't know why, but when Jim would see them, he would point to them and laugh and then show us that they had big bellies. There was never anything on TV showing heavy people let along making jokes about them, so why he would always laugh we have no idea.

When we lived in South Philly, many of our friends and the guys who watched out for Jim were in the comics divisions and some in the string bands that marched in the New Year's Parade. They would come to our house dressed in their costumes to show Jim. He loved it, would watch the parade on TV and go over to Mount Carmel School where the mummers came down second street to entertain the nuns and neighbors. Jim would raise his arms up and down doing the mummers strut the way they did to the mummer's music.

Jim loved Halloween. He would watch us carve out our pumpkin and laugh when we did the eyes, nose, and mouth and make the face.

We would put the pumpkin and baskets of candy on the porch. Jim would sit there, and when kids came, he would smile, laugh, point to their costumes then point to the candy for them to take some.

He really loved being around kids. I think he enjoyed watching them run around, jump, and just all their antics would make him laugh, smile, and point at them. I believe he enjoyed it so much because he wished he could have been able to do all they did.

4

When our parents enrolled Jim in a class for handicapped and retarded children, at first, he hated going; I am not sure if it was because he did not want to be associated with them or because he wanted to be home. One time when the driver came to pick him up, he had a hard time getting Jim up from the concrete pavement, making a comment that he didn't think anyone could get a grip on the pavement like it was a handle.

In time, Jim accepted going because he befriended Alvin who sat next to him at their table. It got to a point where Jim would shake his head no at the lunch our mother made for him. In time he got it across that he wanted the same kind of lunch Alvin would bring to class. Not sure how our mother figured this, but she did and would make Jim the same kind of lunch Alvin had.

One day after class, Jim pointed to Alvin in his class picture and showed us that Alvin was smoking by holding his two fingers up to his mouth and then pulling them away and puffing and pointing to our father's pack of cigarettes.

When we were teenagers, brother Johnny got into a fistfight at the corner of our street with a guy named Bumpsy. There was a large crowd of kids watching when Jim came walking by. Somehow Jim got behind Bumpsy and punched him in the back knocking the wind out of him. I never saw that side of Jim but came to realize that he was going to help John out and did. That ended the fights. One guy grabbed Jim and wouldn't you know our father came down to see what was going on at the same time. So, he grabbed the kid who grabbed Jim, and everyone backed off. That ended that.

Jim was twenty-two when our first child Marianne was born, then Marta and John. Like all people who see babies, he wanted to hold but was afraid because of his limited control of his hands and arms. He would shake his head no when we would motion to him to hold Marianne. In time he did relinquish and attempted to hold her. When we finally got him steady and placed her in his arms, his face lit up and had a big smile when he realized he could do it without hurting her. Afterwards with all three he would make faces at them, tickling them and laughing when they would laugh at him.

Holding my daughter Marianne

Jim would describe my wife Dolores and my children Marianne, Marta, and John by putting his hand up to show their height, so I knew which one he was referring to.

Jim and my daughter Marta

Jim with my son John

He did the same with my grandkids, and when they got older, they would all give him high fives and fist bumps like they did at football games on TV. He always had a big smile when they were around indicating how much he enjoyed them too.

Other than Alvin, if Jim saw or passed one of his classmates in the neighborhood, he would not look or wave back to them. We did not know if it were because he saw himself disabled like them and would not accept the fact he was. He had the perseverance to try to do things like normal people and would never give in until he managed to do so. His determination and patience were unbelievable.

The retarded children in the neighborhood were bused to their school which was located a good distance away in West Philadelphia. The local association proposed to buy a building nearby to use as their school. The families of the kids, including our mother and sister, used to go door-to-door weekly asking for donations in order to help purchase the building. This went on for a long period of time. They used to go with Jim's school friend Alvin's mother.

Then one day when they called Alvin's mother to go canvasing, she told them she will no longer go out asking for donations. She informed them that she found out that a large portion of the money they were collecting was going to the administrators and not toward buying the building. The building never got purchased and the kids had to continue taking the long bus rides to school.

5

The older guys in the neighborhood, tough guys, took to looking after Jim. They used to buy him lunch and took him with them when doing things around the neighborhood.

One day they came to our house for Jim and told my father one of their group members' father had died and they wanted to take Jim with them to the viewing. My father told them that Jim did not have a suit to go to the viewing, which was common to wear at that time. They told my father he did not need a suit, they would go in and out quick, so my father let Jim go with them. When they brought Jim home from the viewing, Jim was wearing a suit and had a big smile pointing to it. They had taken Jim to a local tailor and bought him that suit and would not take any money for it. They all chipped in.

Jim in suit older guys bought

On an occasion when we weren't there, a black team and their fans came to the game and Jim did the time clock. After the game was over Jim was leaving on his scooter to come home. Two black kids beat Jim up and stole his scooter. The older guys caught the kids when they tried to hide under pinball machines in the corner store. When they brought Jim home, he was all cut-up and bruised from the beating. The was Jim's first encounter with black people and it left a long toll on him. After that, when our father drove us someplace and Jim saw a black person, he would look down at the car floor and shake. Since he could not communicate like a normal person, we had no way to explain to him that all black people were not like the ones who beat him and took a toll on him for years—and I mean years—Jim looked forward to going to the rec center and keeping the clock. But after that incident he would shake his head no to doing the clock if a black team were playing and go right home.

I often talked about Jim to Jerry, a black man who I worked with and associated with on the outside. He was very friendly. I told him about Jim's experience with the two black kids who beat him up and stole his scooter and how Jim reacts when he sees a black person.

Jerry wanted to meet him and try to change his outlook. So one time when Jerry came to my house, I took him down to meet Jim. When we came in, Jim would not look at Jerry and got very nervous. Jerry (who had a great smile) walked over to Jim, patted him on the back and held out his hand to Jim. Jim looked up, shook Jerry's hand, and gave him a big smile. That was the ice breaker he needed after all those years.

Also, while at rehab home, a black aide also named Jim (and had a beard) used to help Jim and he even watched football with Jim on TV in his room. I recall coming to see Jim and they were watching football. Jim pointed to him with a smile and indicated to me that he had a beard too. Those two experiences, I believe, had made a big difference on Jim's outlook, and took away a lot of stress from his past interactions.

6

When my parents, Jim and Ann, moved from Philadelphia to the Lansdale area, Jim met a lot of people. In time he used to sit in a chair at the bottom of their driveway in the late afternoon and wave to all the cars passing by; most blew their horn or waved, and some would even stop and shake his hand.

One time when Jim was off somewhere, whoever it was with gave him too much beer. They left Jim off at the bottom of the driveway without telling anyone. Jim managed to crawl up the lawn to the door. Needless to say, our parents were very upset. After that we would kid Jim by showing him a bottle of beer and offering it to him. He would shake his head no, then we would kid him about crawling on the rug. He would laugh knowing what we were referring to.

Jim would walk our dogs. One day when he was out, he apparently stepped into a hole and broke his better leg into two places. He somehow managed to crawl back to the house. My son-in-law Dan was a doctor and he happened to be at the house visiting. When we got Jim into chair, he pointed at Dan to look at his leg; no one else was allowed to, since he apparently knew that Dan was a doctor.

Somehow Jim learned the time on the clock when our parents would point to the number on the clock and then put a finger near their mouth to indicate that's when we would eat. After that they would use the clock to indicate to him when other things would happen i.e., going in the car and showing him steering the wheel when going out in the car.

When our mother could not get out for church anymore, our priest would come to the house after mass and give our mother and Jim Holy Communion. They would point to the clock, show Jim their hands folded like praying (for the priest) when he would be there. One time the priest came later, and Jim pointed to the clock indicating that he was late.

The priest asked what Jim was doing and they told him that Jim was telling him that he was late. He couldn't believe it and pointed to Jim and laughed telling him that he was sorry.

Jim loved to drink Coke and make faces if you offered him something else. When he noticed the Coke was getting low, he would take his wagon and go to the beer distributor, who knew what he wanted, that was about one mile away, get his case and bring it home.

If our parents threw something in the trash that Jim didn't want thrown out, it would show up in his room on the bookshelf or bureau. How he knew or got it, no one's knows.

Aunt Mary, our mother's sister, really treated him special, never missing his birthday and sending him a card with money in it. She was a good seamstress and would repair rips in Jim's clothes that happened a lot along with him pulling buttons from his shirts or pants. When that happened, nobody and I mean nobody could sew the buttons back or darn his socks, etc. … except for Aunt Mary. And Uncle Charlie, who was an auto mechanic, was the only person who could trim Jim's beard. I think because Charlie would tease him if his beard got long and show him the scissors. Jim allowed him to trim his beard, and after that he was the only one allowed to.

Somehow Jim got to know the volunteer firefighters at the local firehouse. One fireman in particular named Bud took Jim under his wing and taught him to show people where to park their cars at various events. They gave Jim a hat and crossing guard chest straps to wear at the events and would point to them and show us his hand signals telling people where to park.

Parking cars at events

With his love for dogs, he used to rip out pictures of dogs in the newspapers or magazine. Our parents even got calendars with different dogs for each month for him and buy dog figures that he lined up on the shelves in his room. And don't dare to rearrange them either. They had their place, and he didn't want anything changed.

When Jim would get sick, he would put his hand on his forehead for our mother to feel it like a normal person would do to see if you may have a fever. He would wave his hand and go to the spot on his shoulder moving his finger indicating he wanted a needle. He apparently felt that getting a needle would cure his sickness from past experiences.

7

Susan, a neighbor of our parents, used to come visit and wound-up teaching Jim the Rock, Paper, Scissors game. It took a long time for him to catch on, but he did. Jim even would beat her at times, and she couldn't believe it. She still mentions it to us that she could not get over him catching on and beating her; she did tell us she did not lose to him on purpose.

I recently met a neighbor who told me when he was younger, he and Jim would sit in his front yard and have a beer. He said they would just sit there, and a lot of joggers would use the trail across from his house and that Jim would put his fingers up counting them. How he learned that or even why he did that I can't explain, but for him to find that counting them must have been entertaining to him.

At times Jim would come with us when we played baseball. He really seemed to enjoy the game. One day we got together to try and get him involved. We motioned to him if he would like to swing the bat, and he shook his head yes. He could only swing the bat in one direction, downward. So, I would pitch the ball to match his swing. He finally hit the ball and ran as best as he could toward first base.

We waited until after he reached first base before throwing the ball. He was elated thinking he got a hit. We allowed the next batters to get hits and point to him to run to second, third, and later home.

When he scored everyone watching cheered and clapped, and he wouldn't stop laughing and smiling.

When we got home, he showed our parents by swinging the bat and running. We told them about the game and allowing him to play and they patted him on the back and praised him with gestures.

When Jim was eligible for social security after our father passed away, we had to take him down to their office every year for them to verify that he was disabled. Later it got harder when Jim was confirmed to a wheelchair; they still had us bring him there every year.

Over time it got very frustrating after our local state representative told us to apply for food stamps for Jim. He was turned down every year. It seemed worse to us because while we waited to be waited on, the office was always filled with refugees who were there speaking in foreign languages and all seemed happy when leaving because they approved for food stamps.

Finally, one year when we brought Jim back to the social security office, the woman waiting on us saw how hard it was for him and asked why we were bringing him there in that condition. We explained to her that the person who always waited on us told us we had to bring him back there physically every year.

She told us that was not right, and she would put it in his file that he no longer had to come every year. He was even approved for food stamps after that.

On Jim's birthday, we would only light one candle because he could not blow all those candles out without spitting all over. For some reason he was not capable of just blowing air like everyone else either.

He would laugh when we lit the candle and show him how old he was by holding up our hands and keep flashing our fingers then point to his shoulder on how many punches he would be getting. He enjoyed opening his presents and really enjoyed opening the envelopes with money in it. I would tease him about holding the money, but he would laugh at me and point to his pocket. Then he would indicate how high his stack of money was now.

When Jim was in the Doylestown hospital being treated for his broken leg, my mother and sister went to visit him, and when they got there, the nurses told them that Jim was a hero and that he saved his roommate's life. His roommate was a man who had a metal brace over his head for a broken neck.

The man had started choking on his lunch, to a point where Jim realized he needed help. Jim got out of his bed somehow into his wheelchair and made his way to the nurses' station for help. They claimed if Jim didn't do that his roommate probably would have not made it.

8

Jim grew a beard and loved it. When I would tease him about shaving it off by pointing to my face, showing him that I shave, he would shake his head no to me. When the show *Duck Dynasty* came on TV, he would watch it intensely, point to his beard and then to the TV with the guys and their beards. He would then place his hands down to his waist indicating he was going to grow it that long.

Every time he saw someone with a beard, he would point to them and then to his beard and shake his head in approval. If you had a beard you were in his good graces.

Jim was not too fond of cats, probably because they were not as friendly as dogs. My son John had a cat and a dog. The cat, Spike, stayed at my parents' house if John had to go away. Spike was really different, always hunting, sitting in someone's lap or going to his favorite spot in the house.

Jim would smile and point to him as though he approved of him even though Spike would never go to him or sit in his lap (Spike must have known Jim didn't care for cats). Not sure if he liked Spike's different ways or because he belonged to John. Also, not sure if Jim's condition had something to do with Spike avoiding him.

Jim could never read or write. We did get him to write his name that looked like this "JIM". He always watched when we were doing out homework or reading a book. I would show him the book I was reading, and he would look at the printed pages then at me and shrug his shoulders and make a face. But when we showed him a comic book, he would look at the pictures intently and even turn the pages to look at the rest of the pictures. My father got the monthly publication of the Pennsylvania Game News that he would look through and smile and point to the deer pictures or drawings.

9

When I went to visit our mother, she was really failing, suffering, in pain and kept saying she had to stay for Jimmy. I told her not to worry, that we would care for him the way she did. She passed away that night.

When Jim went downhill after our mother passed away, we had to move his bed downstairs and had to get him into bed too, change his clothes, put him in his wheelchair and feed him. Jim failed to a point where he could not use the bathroom on his own. We had to get him up and clean him after he had bowel movements. We were surprised that he realized that he needed that help from us especially since he never let you see him in his underwear let along clean him up, change his clothes, and put a diaper on him. Later, we had to put him in for rehabilitation.

Surprisingly, he accepted going there to be taken care of. Ann would go every day at lunch to help him eat and for moral support. I did likewise at suppertime; after supper we watched TV until it was time for them to put him to bed.

Cindy, one of the nurses there, was very outgoing, moved fast, and at times spoke loudly. She would kid with Jim and he really took to her, to a point that they would kid each other by making faces and jesters. I taught Jim to point to his eyes with his two fingers then point at Cindy to show he was watching her. She would laugh and do the same back to Jim and they both would laugh. I am not sure if Jim understood that gesture indicating he was watching her or not, but he seemed to.

As I said, Cindy was loud at times, and if Jim has his back to her but heard, he would get my attention and using his hand gesturing talking then point his thumb to indicate she was behind him and then laugh.

There were many different aides working there, and there were some who understood Jim's condition more than others. On different occasions while I was there, I could tell, by his reactions to them, as to who was good with him and who wasn't by his facial expressions and composure.

They used to get Jim out of bed right before supper then wheel him into the dining hall to eat. Once when I was there, when they brought his food, I started cutting up his meat to feed him. This aide came behind Jim and stated wheeling him away from the table. I asked her what she was doing, and she said putting him to bed. I told her he just got up and was getting to eat his supper. She said he's going to bed now! I had to get the nurse on duty to stop her because she was so nasty. The nurse told her he just got up and it was his suppertime, and he does not go back to bed until about 9:00.

The aide walked off in a huff and I wondered what else she used to do to him when Ann and I were not around. Rosey was a patient there who was always helping the other patients with their food or napkins and with any others issues she saw going on. She took a liking to Jim and would help him and kid with him. Jim would laugh at her and she would stand-up put her hands on her hips and pretend to scold him. She was under five feet tall, and Jim looked down at her sitting in his wheelchair. He would burst out laughing and point to how high she was.

One nurse would push Jim in his wheelchair and joke with him pushing him a little fast, stop, make a hard turn when taking him out of the dining hall. Jim would laugh out loud, shake his head to go and point in what direction as though she didn't know where to go.

He always seemed to know who cared for him and who just wanted to avoid doing their care job so I guess they could go goof off somewhere. And Jim was an easy target since he could not speak. I came to the conclusion about goofing off somewhere based on the same thing that used to happen with our mother when she was in a home. One of the aides there told us that's what they did there, and she was disgusted about that going on.

Beth, who was at the next table to Jim, was another person he enjoyed. She would kid around with Jim, and when I got the best of her, she would shake her fist at me. Jim would break out laughing, look at me and point his thumb at her like "who is she kidding."

Frank, who was blind, sat at another table, used to talk out loud to himself and sing rock and roll songs while smiling and throwing his head about. Jim would look at me nod his head toward Frank and laugh.

As a kid growing up, I learned to draw and had a few drawing classes in high school and college. Many years ago, I did a drawing of a deer in the woods with an insert of my father on it and gave it to him as a Christmas present. Everyone seemed to like it including Jim who nodded his head in approval. Years later, I did one with Jim wearing his hunting hat as an insert. He was thrilled to death and had us hang it up in his bedroom.

After Jim was placed in the rehabilitation home, he motioned to the wall by his bed and got across to us to bring the picture and hang it there. If I was there and an aide or nurse was in there and looked at the drawing, he would grunt to them for their attention then point to me that I did that drawing for him.

Picture I drew for Dad

Picture I drew for Jim

10

Jim shared his table with Larry who did not appear to like his food by the way he ate but would eat all his desserts. We would bring Jim treats and he would nod his head to give Larry some. Apparently, he noticed the same thing about his eating habits as us.

Jim would always look at his food when they placed it in front of him, then nod his head yes or make a face if it didn't look good or appetizing. At various times, they showed movies or some kind of entertainment downstairs and they would take him there, and he seemed to enjoy this diversity. However, as I stated earlier, we watched TV after he ate. He would not go anywhere until *Jeopardy* was over since he always watched that show with our mother.

Even though he showed no signs of failing more, I noticed another change when I brought him his favorite McDonald's sandwich, which he loved to eat (and never turned down). He made a face and motioned he did not want it. Jim passed away one week after that. I felt that it was a sign of him going down, but he couldn't communicate how he was feeling to us.

Since we taught him to write his name, when he had to sign any paperwork, they accepted him just writing "JIM" based on his condition. Toward the end, I got concerned when he started to sign his name as "JIW". He had never done that before.

John and Jim

Ann, Father, Mother, Jim, Lloyd, John

Mother and Jim

Father and Jim

Recreation center